ROAD TRIP ACTIVITIES
and TRAVEL JOURNAL
FOR KIDS

Happy Fox
BOOKS

ROAD TRIP ACTIVITIES

and TRAVEL JOURNAL

FOR KIDS

Written by

Kristy ALPERT

Illustrated by

Tamiko MURMAN

© 2021 by Kristy Alpert and Happy Fox Books, an imprint of
Fox Chapel Publishing Company, Inc., 903 Square Street, Mount Joy, PA 17552.

Road Trip Activities and Travel Journal for Kids is an original work, first published
in 2021 by Fox Chapel Publishing Company, Inc. Reproduction of its contents is
strictly prohibited without written permission from the rights holder.

ISBN 978-1-64124-099-4

To learn more about the other great books from Fox Chapel Publishing,
or to find a retailer near you, call toll-free

800-457-9112 or visit us at www.FoxChapelPublishing.com.

We are always looking for talented authors.
To submit an idea, please send a brief inquiry to
acquisitions@foxchapelpublishing.com.

Fox Chapel Publishing makes every effort to use environmentally friendly paper
for printing.

Printed in Singapore

First printing

You're going on a road trip...

Woohoo! Get ready for an epic adventure! Road trips aren't just about driving to go somewhere new or to arrive at your destination quickly; they're about the thrill of the open road and the freedom to let your mind wander so you can fully enjoy the journey.

This book will be your companion on your road trip, offering ideas for when you get a little bored, but mostly providing ways for you to make the most out of every minute. You'll notice this book is broken down into seven chapters, but feel free to choose your own adventure: skip pages, work ahead, revisit previous chapters, combine multiple days into one, or even rip out pages and save them for your next road trip. This is your book after all; have fun with it!

Road trips are always full of surprises. Along the way, you will likely see new things, meet new people, and maybe even smell or taste something you never even knew existed. Places, signs, and people will zoom past you, and you never know if you will see them again, so keep your eyes open and take in every moment before it passes you by.

And don't forget ... *enjoy the ride!*

Kristy Alpert

Table of Contents

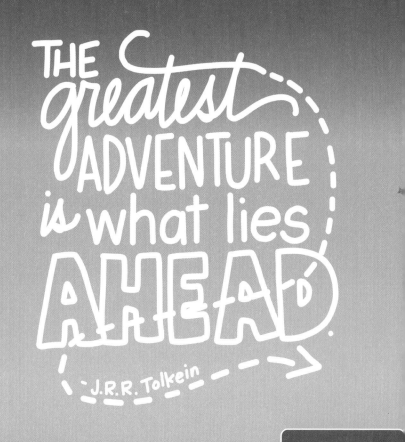

THE
greatest
ADVENTURE
is what lies
AHEAD

-J.R.R. Tolkein

Before
You Go

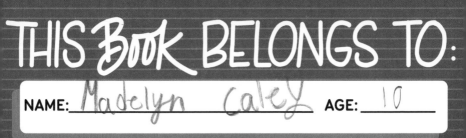

THIS *Book* BELONGS TO:

NAME: Madelyn Caley   **AGE:** 10

Favorite color:
Teal

Favorite food:
Cheeseburger

Favorite number:
8

Secret talent:
Baking

Best friend:
Tenley

How many road trips have you been on before?
3

How many of these destinations have you been to before? Circle them here.

Alabama	Hawaii	Massachusetts	New Mexico	South Dakota
Alaska	Idaho	Michigan	New York	Tennessee
Arizona	Illinois	Minnesota	North Carolina	Texas
Arkansas	Indiana	Mississippi	North Dakota	Utah
California	Iowa	Missouri	Ohio	Vermont
Colorado	Kansas	Montana	Oklahoma	Virginia
Connecticut	Kentucky	Nebraska	Oregon	Washington
Delaware	Louisiana	Nevada	Pennsylvania	West Virginia
Florida	Maine	New Hampshire	Rhode Island	Wisconsin
Georgia	Maryland	New Jersey	South Carolina	Wyoming

Alberta	New Brunswick	Northwest Territories	Ontario	Quebec
British Columbia	Newfoundland and Labrador	Nova Scotia	Prince Edward Island	Saskatchewan
Manitoba		Nunavut		Yukon

USA and CANADA Map →

Draw the route you'll be taking.

(Feel free to ask for help from an adult if you need it!)

ALASKA

YUKON

NORTHWEST TERRITORIES

BRITISH COLUMBIA

ALBERTA

SASKATCHEWAN

WASH-INGTON

OREGON

IDAHO

MONTANA

NOR DAK

SOU DAK

WYOMING

NEBR

CALIFORNIA

NEVADA

UTAH

COLORADO

ARIZONA

NEW MEXICO

TEX

HAWAII

NUNAVUT

MANITOBA

ONTARIO

QUEBEC

NEWFOUNDLAND AND LABRADOR

PRINCE EDWARD ISLAND

NEW BRUNS-WICK

NOVA SCOTIA

MAINE

TH OTA

TH OTA

MINNESOTA

WISCONSIN

MI-CHI-GAN

NEW YORK

VERMONT

NEW HAMPSHIRE

MASSA-CHUSETTS

RHODE ISLAND

CONNECTICUT

ASKA

IOWA

ILLINOIS

INDIANA

OHIO

PENN-SYLVANIA

NEW JERSEY

MARYLAND

DELAWARE

KANSAS

MISSOURI

WEST VIRGINIA

VIRGINIA

OKLA-HOMA

ARKANSAS

TENNESSEE

KENTUCKY

N. CAROLINA

S. CAROL-INA

AS

LOUISIANA

MISSISSIPPI

ALABAMA

GEORGIA

FLORIDA

11

WHERE I'M GOING

Destination: Kitty Hawk

Date I'm leaving: 8/28/21   **Date I'm returning:** 9/4/21

These are the people coming with me: Mom, Dad, Ethan, Ryan, Michelle Aot, lisa, and their kids

This is the type of vehicle I'll be riding in:
Explorer

I can't wait to eat:
Shacks

Draw what you're most excited to see:

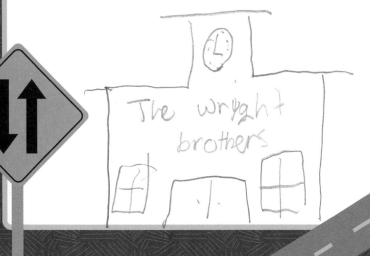

The wright brothers

ABOUT YOUR DESTINATION

Have you been there before?
[CIRCLE ONE]

Yup   ⟨Nope⟩

Answer the following questions:
(It's okay to ask an adult for help!)

What will the weather be like there?

Hot and sunny

What are some famous sights/attractions where you're going?

The wright brothers musean

What is the state bird at your destination?

What will you do when you get there?

Unpack and swim in the pool

Did you know that every U.S. state has its own motto? A motto is a short phrase that represents the intentions, ideals, or goals of the people living within that state. Think about what intentions you may have for your road trip, and then write your own motto for the trip below.

All for the adventure.

"FREEDOM and UNITY" – Vermont

"One DEFENDS and the other CONQUERS" – Nova Scotia

"ALL for our COUNTRY" – Nevada

WHAT I'M BRINGING

Shoes, socks, swimsuits ... there are lots of things you need while traveling. What will you be bringing? Draw in those items here.

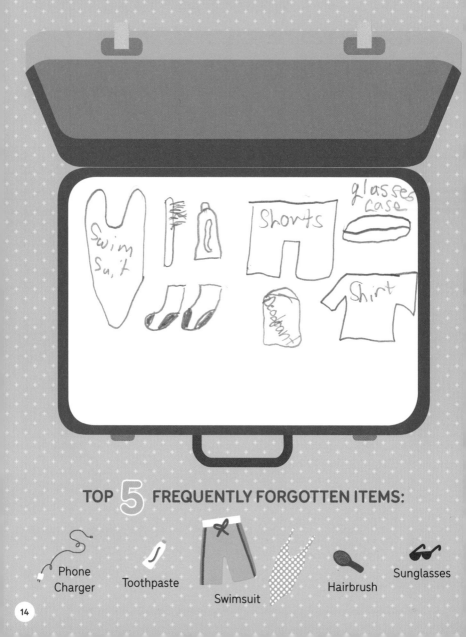

TOP 5 FREQUENTLY FORGOTTEN ITEMS:

Phone Charger

Toothpaste

Swimsuit

Hairbrush

Sunglasses

CREATE THE *Ultimate* ROAD TRIP PLAYLIST

Every great road trip needs an awesome soundtrack. Music helps set the mood for the entire journey, and scientists have proven that music can actually help you remember the trip once you are back home. So cool, right?! Use this form to help you create the ultimate road trip playlist.

List 3 songs that make you happy.
1. waitress sad
2.
3.

List 3 songs that you love to sing along to.
1.
2.
3.

List 3 songs that make you want to dance.
1.
2.
3.

List 3 songs that the other passengers would like.
1.
2.
3.

List 3 songs you definitely don't want to hear on the trip.
1.
2.
3.

Bonus!

List one song from another decade.

List one song that has the word "car" in it.

ROAD TRIP *Fuel*

WHAT YOU'LL NEED:

1 Large bowl

Measuring cups

1 Large sealable bag/jar or 7 small sealable bags/jars

INGREDIENTS:

1 cup of something salty, like ...

- ☐ Nuts
- ☐ Roasted chickpeas
- ☐ Wasabi peas
- ☐ Pretzels

1/2 cup of something chewy, like ...

- ☐ Raisins
- ☐ Dried cranberries
- ☐ Dried goji berries
- ☐ Candied ginger

1 cup of something crunchy, like ...

- ☐ Goldfish®
- ☐ Pre-popped popcorn
- ☐ Cereal (Chex®, Cheerios®, Cinnamon Toast Crunch®, etc.)
- ☐ Banana chips or apple chips

1/4 cup of something small, like ...

- ☐ Sunflower seeds
- ☐ Pumpkin seeds
- ☐ Coconut flakes
- ☐ Cocoa nibs

1/4 cup of something sweet, like ..

- ☐ Freeze dried strawberries
- ☐ Mini marshmallows
- ☐ Bite-sized cookies
- ☐ Candy corn

Just like a car needs fuel to drive, you'll need fuel while on the road, too. There will be lots of chances to try new foods on the trip, but having a handy snack to nibble on will give you energy between stops. Trail mix is the ultimate road trip snack, and it's easy to make at home from ingredients you already have. Follow the recipe below, and feel free to get creative with the foods you choose for your personal "road trip fuel!" Makes 3 cups.

Adjust as needed for anyone with food allergies on the trip.

FUN FACT:

Some of the first trail mixes were mixed with berries and dried buffalo meat.

DIRECTIONS:

Combine all of your chosen ingredients into a large bowl and stir with your hands or a spoon to mix it up. Transfer the mix into a large sealable bag or a reusable container, or divide the mix into 7 smaller sealable bags or reusable containers. [TIP: leave the chocolate at home; chocolate can melt in hot cars and will fuel a mess instead of fueling you!]

Trail mix goes by lots of names around the world, like "Scroggin," "GORP," "Ajil," and "Student Fodder."

What will you call your creation?

Adventures
I WANT TO HAVE

- Try a new food
- Sleep outside under the stars
- Take a selfie in front of a National Landmark
- Search for hidden treasure
- Swim in a lake or river
- Do a cartwheel in an open field
- Bury my legs in sand or snow
- Tour a cave
- Go whitewater rafting
- See wild animals
- Ride in a go-kart
- Go horseback riding
- Paint a picture outside
- Ride in a hot air balloon
- Build a sandcastle or a snow cave
- Slide down a sand dune
- Yell as loud as I can from the top of a mountain
- See a waterfall

- Learn a new dance
- Have a water battle
- Volunteer at an animal sanctuary
- Climb a tree
- Have a snail race
- Roll down a hill
- Plant a tree
- Catch a firefly and set it free
- Fly a kite
- Pet a farm animal
- Skip stones on the water
- Watch the sunrise or sunset
- Hike to the top of a hill
- Use a compass
- Make a new friend
- Ride in a tractor
- Stand over a state line to be in two places at once

DAILY JOURNAL

Write a letter to yourself about what you hope will happen on this trip.

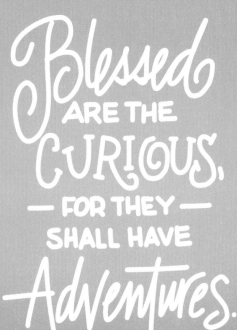

Blessed
ARE THE
CURIOUS,
— FOR THEY —
SHALL HAVE
Adventures.
[often attributed to]
-Lovelle Drachman

Chapter One

TRAVEL LOG

Date: _____

Today we started in _____
                                    NAME OF CITY

and traveled _____ miles to _____.
              # OF MILES   DESTINATION CITY

My favorite stop was:

DRAWING of the DAY:

FAVORITE Food OF THE DAY:

TODAY'S Weather:

Highlight OF THE DAY:

SPOT IT!

- Fire truck that is *not* red
- Flag raised halfway on a flagpole
- Window decal from a college
- Delivery truck
- Someone with a flat tire
- Cow under a tree
- Round hay bale
- Building with more than five stories
- Abandoned building
- Someone picking their nose while driving
- "Speed Limit Enforced by Aircraft" sign
- Someone fishing
- Boat trailer
- Horse trailer with horses inside
- Barking dog

- License plate from a state you've never visited
- Park bench
- Statue of a person
- "For Sale" sign
- Bug on the windshield
- Basketball hoop
- Red curb
- Swimming pool
- Cemetery
- Someone dancing in a car
- Fuzzy dice
- Billboard with an animal on it
- Baseball diamond
- Someone waiting at a bus stop
- "Detour" sign

RIP
RIP

FOR SALE

WOOF

SPEED LIMIT ENFORCED BY AIRCRAFT

DETOUR

Imagination STATION

Notice the windows on the buildings that you're passing. Behind every single window, there is a story. People work there, children live there, or maybe even animals sleep there. The next time you pass a building, choose one window and imagine what might be going on behind it.

Did you know?

Windshield wipers were first invented for trolley cars. Inventor Mary Anderson earned the patent for her "windshield-clearing device" in 1903. Her invention removed snow or rain from the windshield with a rubber blade controlled by a lever inside the trolley. Before her invention was adapted for automobiles in 1923, drivers had to open their windows to be able to see during bad weather.

UNSCRAMBLE THESE WORDS

nisspgot _ _ _ _ _ _ _ _ _

reivd _ _ _ _ _

ernoyuj _ _ _ _ _ _ _

aspergens _ _ _ _ _ _ _ _ _ _

ANSWERS ON PAGE 94

DID YOU KNOW?

The most popular pet in North America isn't a dog or a cat. It's a fish!

Photo SCAVENGER HUNT

Challenge someone else in your vehicle—or just challenge yourself—to this photo scavenger hunt. Simply snap a photo of an item below and cross it off your list. Whoever has the most by the end of the trip wins!

HINT: For each of these, that "someone" can always be you!

1 A spiderweb	**2** Someone balancing a stack of quarters on the back of their hand	**3** Something frozen	**4** A bug without wings	**5** Something fuzzy
6 Someone putting spare change in a donation jar	**7** A cloud in the shape of an animal	**8** Someone smelling a rose	**9** Someone jumping	**10** Something red
11 Someone wearing something with feathers	**12** Someone sleeping in a car	**13** Someone cleaning up a piece of litter	**14** Something with a hole in it	**15** Someone modeling sunglasses
16 Animal footprints	**17** Someone impersonating a statue	**18** Someone else taking a photo	**19** A shadow	**20** Your name spelled out in twigs or sticks
21 A cow	**22** A street sign with the same name as someone you know	**23** Someone doing a cartwheel or handstand in an open field	**24** Someone's toes dipping in water	**25** Someone holding a copy of today's newspaper

Challenge!
Build a boat with only materials you find in nature.

TIE BREAKER:
Whoever was able to stack the most quarters on their hand for **2**

24

COLOR QUEST

The human eye can see more shades of green than any other color. It's true; just ask a scientist. Oh, what? You don't have a scientist in the car? Then let's test it out.

1. First, rub your hands together really, really fast for five seconds and then cover your eyes with the palms of your hands.

2. Then close your eyes and try to feel the warmth from your hands on your eyes for five seconds. (This gives your eyes a little break so you can have a fresh perspective once they reopen.)

3. Now quickly remove your hands and open your eyes and try to only spot green things. You can look outside the window, in the car, or even on your clothes.

Now try it with a different color.

RIDDLE ME THIS

1. What travels around the world yet only stays in one corner?
2. If a red house is made of red bricks, and an orange house is made of orange bricks, what is a greenhouse made of?
3. Which is heavier, a pound of rocks or a pound of feathers?
4. What runs but never walks, murmurs but never talks, has a bed but never sleeps, and has a mouth but never eats?
5. What gets left behind each time you make more?
6. What has no eyes, no ears, and no legs, but helps move the earth?
7. Where do you find cities, towns, shops, and streets, but no people?

ANSWERS ON PAGE 94

DAILY JOURNAL

Become a Travel Writer. Travel writers go all around the world to write their stories. Good travel writers can paint a picture in your head of the place they're describing by only using their words. Describe one place you discovered today (it can even be the back seat of the car) but describe it like a painting. What color was the sky? Did the ground have a different texture? Then use all your senses to describe the rest of the place. What did the air smell like? Did you taste anything new? What did you feel while you were there?

"THE MOST IMPORTANT *reason* FOR GOING FROM *one place to another* IS TO SEE WHAT'S *in between.*"

— NORTON JUSTER, *The Phantom Tollbooth*

Chapter Two

TRAVEL LOG

Date: _____

Today we started in _____
NAME OF CITY

and traveled _____ miles to _____.
OF MILES   DESTINATION CITY

My favorite stop was:

DRAWING of the DAY:

FAVORITE *Food* OF THE DAY:

TODAY'S *Weather*:

Highlight OF THE DAY:

License Plates
FROM ALL THE STATES

All the states, provinces, territories, and districts in the U.S. and Canada have their own unique license plates. Some are green, some have pictures on them, and some Canadian license plates are even shaped like polar bears! Keep track of the license plates you see along the trip by coloring them in below.

Alabama	ALASKA	ARIZONA	Arkansas	California	COLORADO
Connecticut	DELAWARE	FLORIDA	GEORGIA	HAWAII	IDAHO
ILLINOIS	INDIANA	IOWA	KANSAS	Kentucky	Louisiana
MAINE	Maryland	Massachusetts	MICHIGAN	Minnesota	MISSISSIPPI
MISSOURI	MONTANA	NEBRASKA	NEVADA	New HAMPSHIRE	New Jersey
NEW MEXICO	NEW YORK	NORTH CAROLINA	NORTH DAKOTA	OHIO	OKLAHOMA
OREGON	PENNSYLVANIA	Rhode Island	SOUTH CAROLINA	South Dakota	Tennessee
TEXAS	UTAH	Vermont	VIRGINIA	WASHINGTON	WASHINGTON, D.C.
West Virginia	WISCONSIN	WYOMING	Alberta	British Columbia	Manitoba
New Brunswick	Newfoundland & Labrador	NORTHWEST TERRITORIES	NOVA SCOTIA	NUNAVUT	Ontario
Prince Edward Island	Québec	Saskatchewan	Yukon		

78-161
IDAHO POTATOES-1928

Did You Know?

The first image to appear on a license plate was a picture of a potato in 1928.

Design Your Own
LICENSE PLATE

In 1901 the state of New York became the first state to require vehicles to have license plates, but now every state requires registered vehicles to have them. All vehicles today are registered to their owner's home state and assigned a specific number and letter combination for their plates. But in the early days, people just made their own license plates by printing their initials or favorite numbers on wooden or leather boards.

If you could design your own license plate, what letters, numbers, or images would you have on it? Design it here!

The letters I, O, and Q are rarely used on license plates because they are easily mistaken for numbers.

A vanity plate is a registered license plate that has been customized by the vehicle's owner with a personalized message. Can you figure out what these vanity plates mean?

PB4WEGO	L8RBRO	EZRDR	2CSTRZ	GURSLO	ILUVPZA	CR8Z4U

ANSWERS ON PAGE 94

You're a Poet
YOU JUST DIDN'T KNOW IT!

Poems can express your feelings, thoughts, or observations in just a few words. Did you know that not all poems have to rhyme? Some do, but other poems simply shape the words themselves into an object or make "word music" by using sensory words like *buzz*, *crumple*, or *swoosh*. Try out these different types of poems and then see if you can create your own.

RHYMING POEM

Write as many words you can think of that rhyme with "car."
[Hint: there are more than 100!] *bar har*
tar

Now plug some of your "car" rhymes into this poem:

I once had a car

Whose name was _*tar*_

It had a cool _*bar*_

And made the sound _*har*_

I hope it will always _*rar*_ _*bar*_

SIMILE POEM

Use "like" or "as" to describe someone you met or saw today.

As silly/quiet as a monkey/mouse
CIRCLE ONE   CIRCLE ONE

Tall/short like a tree/stump
CIRCLE ONE   CIRCLE ONE

As strong/sweet as a brick/honey
CIRCLE ONE   CIRCLE ONE

_____
THE PERSON YOU SAW / MET

ALLITERATION POEM

Write down the first letter of your name, and then use that same letter or beginning sound as many times as you can in one sentence to describe the vehicle you're riding in.
Example: "The grey gas guzzler glides great on gravelly ground."

_____

_____

_____

RHYTHMIC POEM

Sing this rhythm in your head, and then write your own words that go to the beat.

LA de-dah, LA de-dah, LA LA LA

Example: Off I go, really slow, to the show.

_____/_____/_____

COLOR POEM

Write a poem about all things blue!

Blue.

Blue is ___sky___, ___water___,

and ___rain___.

Blue tastes like _____.

Blue smells like _____.

Blue sounds like _____.

Blue feels like _____.

Blue looks like _____.

Blue makes me _____.

Blue is _____.

Write a poem that fits inside this tire about the wheels on the car.

Write a poem (in any style you want) about the first place you stopped today.

WORD SEARCH

Try to find all the hidden words about your road trip!
Remember, words can be diagonal, vertical, and horizontal.

```
w a z v b f u x a z e t s n t y n n c w
r r n x e h a j r f e t h m i l e a g e
g o j j a i g l x w f n i i i v m j e l
f w a x b l t n r b p f g w s e h d m b
t x w d x x p k c l l b j i f x i b t w
g r l e t e e u s i f t a b n g s p j m
q z a i r r y p r d m w q d k e i e s k
f k j v d u i o m g k b d l e g h r j v
q u o f e q n p t o a k c g d g z z q k
e d u s r l k p u s t s j p o t h o l e
f x u d f v a u j g p e h j w w k b c g
g b c l o z q k e f c e l r e c i l a v
g m o t o r c y c l e u e i f x o b r v
x d t c q m g u s e u g j d c g o b j o
q p c e q l b s n q a m d o l e e q u o
m g t j n n c e m z a r o j u i n s k n
z d r i v e r b m m o a y f j r m s h y
p f u a v j q a c a c d h x s z n i e n
l q c v l f r t q y p i t j f o m e t t
z a k v l r q q p e l o b s g k b u y p
```

motorcycle   speed limit   road trip   journey
pothole   license   mileage   travel
driver   engine   motel   truck
radio   gas   map   car

34   ANSWERS ON PAGE 93

WOULD YOU RATHER?

Ride a rollercoaster or swim in a lake?

Go camping or sleep on a boat?

Not be able to smell or not be able to smile?

Own a pet sea otter or a pet fox?

Sweat mayonnaise or drool mustard?

Only wear a swimsuit the rest of your life or

only wear a snow suit the rest of your life?

Be able to fly or be able to breathe under water?

Sneeze every time an hour passes or

fall asleep for five minutes every three hours?

Have hands instead of feet or feet instead of hands?

Eat hot dogs for breakfast or pancakes for dinner?

Know your future or know what everyone is thinking?

Jump in a pool of noodles or a pool of chocolate pudding?

Have a pouch like a kangaroo or a tail like an opossum?

Be a professional race car driver or a professional surfer?

PHOTO CHALLENGE:

Spell out your name using photos you take throughout the trip. Simply take a close-up picture of something that looks like each letter in your name—like twigs in the shape of a "Y," metal beams on a bridge that look like an "A," big bold letters on a billboard, etc.—and then compile and print out the pictures when you get home to spell out your name. Place the photos side-by-side in a frame for a cool wall hanging in your room.

WHAT'S THAT *Smell*?

Did you know the human nose can smell 1 trillion different scents? There are 128 scent molecules that all mix together in different patterns to form the smells we know, like freshly-cut grass, hot rubber, tall pine trees, and BBQ smoke.

Take a deep breath in and out, and then roll the window down and count how many different scents your nose can pick up. Write them down in the first area to the right. Wait one hour and try again, writing down each smell in the second area.

FIRST WHIFF:

SECOND WHIFF:

SCENTS or CENTS?

Homophones are words that are pronounced the same, but have different meanings or spellings, like two and too, fair and fare, sweet and suite. Can you come up with five more?

1.
2.
3.
4.
5.

DAILY JOURNAL

Pretend you are a grasshopper that hopped on the vehicle for the entire day today. Describe all the things you saw, starting when you landed on the windshield.

Today I jump on one of those giant metal moving object. I hoped on the invisible force that keeps me from getting inside. And I just stayed there like an hour. Then I explored. The thing was black, so it was very hot. But I managed to move around. It was very boring but windy because this big object was moving fast! Then I was getting forced to the front and went into this vent looking thing where it was less windy but hot air was going out. Then I saw a giant machine!

To be continued

TRAVEL LOG

Date: 8/28/21

Today we started in __Dillisburg__
NAME OF CITY

and traveled __300+__ miles to __Kitty Hawk__.
OF MILES   DESTINATION CITY

My favorite stop was:
Dunkin Donuts

DRAWING of the DAY:

FAVORITE Food OF THE DAY:
Reeses cup bar

TODAY'S Weather:

Highlight OF THE DAY:
Riding in the car

MAKE A

Use bendable twigs or stems from weeds or flowers that you find along your journey—at rest stops, open fields, campgrounds, etc.—to make the ultimate road trip souvenir!

Step-1: STARTING the RING

Take one long stem or bendable twig (no shorter than the length of your hand) and then bend it to form a loop that's about the same circumference of your finger (the one you want to wear the ring on). Make sure the two tail ends of the stem extend from the circle just a bit.

Step-2: CREATING the BASE

Pinch the point where the two tail ends come together, and then cross them before taking one tail end and wrapping it over and under the circle a few times until it stays in place and you can't wrap any more.

Then do the same thing with the other tail end. It's okay if some of the tail ends stick up once they're wrapped in place ... they will fold down once you add more layers to your ring.

Road Trip Ring

Step 3: ADDING NEW LAYERS

Stick another long stem or bendable twig through the circle, and then start weaving over and under the circle. You'll find that the ring holds itself together by tension when you add more stems or sticks to it, so add as many new stems or bendable twigs that you find along the journey until yours is just right!

Step 4: SHARING YOUR SKILLS!

Once you've mastered your first ring, try making a ring from one stop and then give it away to someone you meet at the next stop!

SEATBACK *Storyteller*

Everyone loves a good story; and telling one can be even more fun than hearing one!

Some stories are silly, and some are sweet, but all good stories have these five things:

✓ **SETTING:** Where the story takes place.
✓ **CHARACTERS:** Who is in the story.
✓ **PLOT:** What is actually happening during the beginning, middle, and end of the story.
✓ **CONFLICT:** A problem or challenge that the characters have to solve.
✓ **RESOLUTION:** The solution to the conflict.

Don't know where to start? See if these story starters can help inspire your next tale.

TEAM STORYTELLING

Take turns with the other people in the car telling one sentence of a story. The first person sets up the story in one sentence, and then starts the next sentence for someone else to finish. Continue taking turns adding to the story until your hilarious tale comes to an end and it's time to start another one!

Example:
Person 1: "Once upon a time there was a dog named Toby who loved licking ice cream cones. But then one day ..."
Person 2: "Someone hid a dog treat inside of an ice cream cone, so when Toby started licking it ..."

LICENSE PLATE STORY STARTERS

Pick three letters from the next license plate you see, and start a sentence using three words that begin with those letters. For example:

California
GJE 631

Greg **J**uggled **E**veryday, but today wasn't like every other day. Today, something big was about to happen, and Greg knew it the minute he ...

RIDDLE ME THIS!

What building has thousands of stories?

ANSWER ON PAGE 94

"ALL GREAT LITERATURE IS ONE OF TWO STORIES; A MAN GOES ON A JOURNEY OR A STRANGER COMES TO TOWN." — *Leo Tolstoy*

ROAD TRIP Bingo

Put an X over any items you see while in the car. You win when you cross out five connecting boxes diagonally, vertically, or horizontally!

Out of state license plate	Bike rack	Exit sign	Bridge	Police car
Wind turbine	Driver wearing a hat	Helicopter	Railroad crossing	Deer
Motorcycle	Tire tracks	FREE SPACE	Construction worker	Traffic light
Mile marker sign	Traffic cone	Billboard	Ambulance	Power lines
Green car	Baby On Board sign	American flag	Water tower	BBQ restaurant

THE DOT GAME

Take turns with another player drawing a single line between two neighboring dots horizontally or vertically. The player who makes a box with their turn earns one point and takes another turn. Put your initial in any boxes you create so you can count up who has the most in the end. The player with the most boxes is the winner!

DAILY JOURNAL

The author Pico Iyer once said, "Travel is not really about leaving our homes, but leaving our habits." What are some of the habits you had at home that you are not doing while on this road trip? Do you think you'll go back to those habits once you return home? Why or why not?

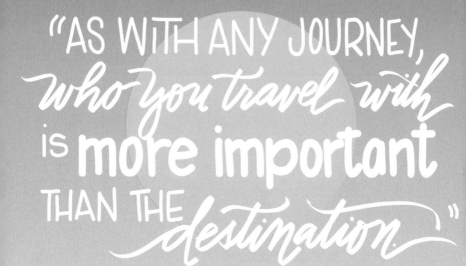

"AS WITH ANY JOURNEY, who you travel with is **more important** THAN THE *destination.*"

— UNKNOWN

Chapter
Four

TRAVEL LOG

Date: _____

Today we started in _____
                                        NAME OF CITY

and traveled _____ miles to _____ .
                    # OF MILES   DESTINATION CITY

My favorite stop was:

FAVORITE *Food* OF THE DAY:

DRAWING *of the* DAY:

TODAY'S *Weather*:

Highlight OF THE DAY:

MAKE A Grass Whistle

At your next stop, find a wide blade of grass that's at least as long as your thumb. Place the blade of grass between your thumbs with your knuckles facing toward you and the heels of your hands touching. Pull the grass tight so you can see the blade straight in the center of the gap between your thumbs. Now just bring the whistle to your mouth and blow!

Different types of grass make different sounds.

A grass whistle isn't really even a whistle … it's a **reed instrument**.

Cupping your hands will **change the pitch** of your whistle either higher or lower.

Did you know there is an **international whistle code**? Blowing on a whistle three times for three seconds per blow means "help me!"

Silly Fill-Ins:
THE ROAD TRIP GONE WRONG

Without reading the story, ask a friend or fellow passenger to provide an answer for each missing word or phrase below. Fill in the answers as you go, and then read the story out loud once you've finished.

We were driving in our ___Jeep___ on our way to
___Beach___, when all of a sudden we heard a loud
TYPE OF VEHICLE
PLACE
___Thunder___. ___Ethan___ stepped out but couldn't see
TYPE OF NOISE   NAME OF PERSON IN CAR
anything because of his/her ___Smelly___ ___tree___, so
                              ADJECTIVE   NOUN
I got out to help find the problem. All of the tires were flat! There
was a/an ___fancy___ rock in the middle of the road, and pieces
          ADJECTIVE
of ___fat___ ___spare tire___ under the tires. We called a tow
   ADJECTIVE   NOUN
truck, but had to wait ___356,289___ hours before it could come, so we
                        NUMBER
went to ___Roy Roger___ to order ___Shrimp___. They were all
        RESTAURANT NAME   TYPE OF FOOD
out of ___candy___, and the only flavor of pie they had was
       TYPE OF FOOD
___pickles___ pie! We ordered water and drank it ___slowly___
NOUN   ADVERB
before going back to meet the tow truck driver. He said,
"___hey___, I've never seen a ___shoelace___ so ___portly___!"
  INTERJECTION   NOUN   ADJECTIVE
That's when we all knew, this was the ___horridy___ road trip ever!
                                       SUPERLATIVE

NOUN: a person, place, thing, or idea
ADJECTIVE: describes a noun

VERB: action word
ADVERB: describes a verb

INTERJECTION: an exclamation, like "egads," "yikes," or "woohoo!"
SUPERLATIVE: an extreme adjective describing a noun, like "worst," "best," or "happiest"

IN THEIR SHOES

Even if you're spending most of your time in the car with the same people, there are so many new people you're seeing each day. The kid in the car you passed by yesterday probably has a best friend back home, and that waitress you ordered dinner from possibly listens to the same music you do. Just because someone lives in a different place doesn't mean they're that different from you. All humans sleep, eat, and dream.

IN THIS SHOE, LIST OUT WHAT A TYPICAL DAY LOOKS LIKE FOR YOU AT HOME, STARTING WITH THE TIME YOU NORMALLY WAKE UP IN BED.

The average person owns

19 PAIRS OF SHOES.

How many pairs of shoes do you own?

IN THIS SHOE, WRITE OUT WHAT YOU IMAGINE A TYPICAL DAY LOOKS LIKE FOR SOMEONE YOU SAW TODAY.

Certain words can give hints to where a person is from. For instance, most Midwesterners call a carbonated beverage "pop," while people from the Northeast call it "soda" and Southerners call it "coke."

DO YOU SAY...

Coke, Soda, or Pop?
Sneakers or Tennis Shoes?
Sub or Hoagie?
Garage Sale, Tag Sale, Rummage Sale, or Yard Sale?
You Guys or Y'all?
Garbage Can or Trash Can?
Drinking Fountain, Water Fountain, or Bubbler?
Eighteen-Wheeler, Semitruck, or Tractor Trailer?
Fireflies or Lightning Bugs?

YOU ATE WHAT?

MENU

Match These Funky Foods with Their Descriptions

1. Koolickles
2. Fry Sauce
3. Scrapple
4. Loco Moco
5. Boudin
6. Ambrosia Salad
7. Possum Pie
8. Poutine
9. Beavertails
10. Ladyfingers

ANSWER ON PAGE 94

A) Dessert layered with whipped cream, chocolate fudge, and sweetened cream cheese on a pecan shortbread crust

B) A baked loaf of pork, grains, and spices mixed together

C) Pickles soaked in Kool-Aid

D) A type of sausage

E) Ketchup mixed with mayonnaise

F) French fries topped with cheese curds and brown gravy

G) Mix of orange slices, marshmallow fluff, cherries, nuts, coconut flakes, and sugar

H) Fried flat dough dusted in cinnamon and sugar

I) Long thin sponge cakes

J) White rice topped with a hamburger, a fried egg, and brown gravey

Draw a picture of a new food you've tried so far on the trip. Bonus points for anything bizarre!

Imagination STATION

WHAT'S DIFFERENT? Can you identify 5 differences?

ANSWERS ON PAGE 94

Did you know that grass is edible for humans? It's true … but it doesn't taste very good. However, if grass were made out of candy, you'd see a lot more people eating it. Which candy would you pick to replace all the grass? Now look out the window and try to imagine which other candies you'd replace all the things you see. Draw your ideas below.

marshmallow clouds!

chocolate buildings!

cotton candy trees!

Smarties   grass!

53

TIC TACTOE

DAILY JOURNAL

Describe the people you're traveling with on this road trip like they are characters in a movie. What do they look like? What makes them unique? What makes them laugh the hardest? Do they have any secret talents?

"FIND *happiness* BY ENJOYING THE JOURNEY, NOT BY *awaiting* THE DESTINATION."

—PETER SHEPPARD SKÆRYED

Chapter
Five

TRAVEL LOG

Date: _____

Today we started in _____
                                            NAME OF CITY

and traveled _____ miles to _____ .
                    # OF MILES   DESTINATION CITY

My favorite stop was:

DRAWING of the DAY:

FAVORITE Food OF THE DAY:

TODAY'S Weather:

Highlight OF THE DAY:

RAINBOW CARS

Did you know that white cars make up nearly 39 percent of all cars in the world? Not only that, but white, black, silver, and gray actually make up 77 percent of all cars in North America. Not a lot of colorful options, right? Even though they're less common, colorful cars exist, and you'll likely see an entire rainbow of them while you're on the road.

Put these colors in order as you'd see them in a rainbow:
BLUE, RED, ORANGE, GREEN, YELLOW, PURPLE

1 _Red_   4 _green_
2 _orange_   5 _blue_
3 _yellow_   6 _purple_

See if you can find a car in every color of the rainbow. Sound too easy? Here's the trick: the cars must be found in the order of the rainbow's colors. So only after you spot a red car can you start looking for an orange car. Make this a race with the other passenger(s) to see who can complete their rainbow first!

Color can influence how foods taste. Scientists poured the same hot chocolate into a white mug, a cream mug, a red mug, and an orange mug. People who drank from the cups said the chocolate in the cream and orange colored mugs tasted better.

The world's longest-lasting rainbow appeared for six hours on March 14, 1994.

There's a name for the dark gray color you see right after the lights turn off: eigengrau.

When displayed together, the colors and yellow can actually make you hungry.

58

Interview WITH A PASSENGER

Pretend you're a journalist working on a story about the importance of road trips, and interview someone in the car. Use the interview questions below to gather quotes for your story or make up your own questions. Remember, a good journalist always asks follow-up questions!

State your full name:

Where are you from?

Have you ever taken a road trip before? If so, tell me about a favorite memory

from one you've taken.

Name 5 things you would never leave home without when you're on going on a

road trip.

If money or time were not factors, where would you go for your dream road trip

and who would you go with?

CAR YOGA

Sitting for a long time isn't easy on your body, and it can leave you feeling stiff, restless, or even stir crazy. Yoga is a great way to get some movement in your body, and you can even do some yoga poses while in the car! Make sure you're buckled in and get moving with these car yoga poses.

UJJAYI BREATH

Ujjayi [pronounced ooh-JAI-yee] means "victorious breath" in Sanskrit, and it's a breathing technique that boosts your energy and strengthens your brain power. Amazing, right?! Start by sitting up straight and bringing one hand in front of your face with your palm facing toward your mouth. Inhale deeply through your nose, and then, as you exhale out your mouth, pretend like your hand is a mirror and try to fog it up with your breath. Now take another breath in through your nose, but this time close your lips halfway through your exhale. Hear that hissing sound from the back of your throat? That's your ujjayi breath! Lower your hand now and practice a few ujjayi breaths on your own, inhaling through your nose and exhaling with your lips closed for a full ujjayi breath. Repeat as often as you'd like on the road trip, or any time you need a little power boost!

SEATED SIDE STRETCH
("Parsva Sukhasana" in Sanskrit)

Inhale as you lift your arms up as high as you can, then grab one of your wrists with the opposite hand and lean over to the side of the hand doing the grabbing. Allow your neck to relax and make sure your hips are level and rooted in your seat. Take four deep breaths in this pose and then rise back up to the center when you're done. Now do the same thing on the other side.

SEATED SUN SALUTATION
("Surya Namaskar" in Sanskrit)

Start by sitting up straight and bringing your hands to a prayer position in the center of your chest with your thumbs facing toward you.

Inhale while bringing your arms up as high as you can ...

... and then exhale as you lean forward at the waist (as far as you're able to go with a seat belt on), keeping your back straight while you come into a forward fold. Let your arms and head relax down to the floor.

Inhale while you slightly lift up and place your hands on your shins, and then exhale while you fold back over.

Inhale while returning to a sitting up position and reach your arms back up in the air.

Exhale while bringing your hands back to the prayer position in front of your chest. That's one sun salutation. Feel free to do as many as you'd like.

What is Sanskrit?

Sanskrit is one of the oldest languages in the world and is the original language of yoga. Very few people speak the language today, but the Sanskrit names of the yoga poses are often still used in yoga classes out of respect for yoga's history.

Our favorite Sanskrit word is
GOMUKHASANA
[go-moo-KAH-sah-nah], mainly because it means "cow face pose" ... and, let's be honest, cows are funny.

DID YOU HEAR THAT?

Have you ever been told that you have "selective hearing," or "you only hear what you want to hear?" Well, it may actually be true! By focusing on certain sounds, you can control your hearing kind of like how you control the volume on the TV or radio ... it just takes a little practice. Put your skills to the test with this hearing game.

1. Start by rolling down the window (it's best to get permission from the driver first, especially if it's raining).

2. Once the window is down, close your eyes and take a deep breath in through your nose for five seconds and then exhale through your nose for five seconds. Keep that breath pattern going while you try to listen to everything you hear outside of the car. Listen for birds chirping, car horns honking, the constant hum of the wind, etc., but only listen to sounds happening outside of the car.

3. With the window still down, imagine that you have a volume control on your hearing and try to turn down every sound you just heard outside the car. All you're left with now are the sounds happening inside the car. Maybe you hear the radio, maybe someone is talking, or maybe you just hear the sounds of the suitcases bouncing together as you hit bumps in the road.

4. This time you're going to turn down all those sounds inside the car as well, so that they're so low you can almost hear your own heart beating. It may help to close your eyes or put your hand over your heart so you can feel it beat. See how long you can go before you start to turn back up the volume of those other sounds in the car.

5. Now turn back up the volume on the sounds happening outside the car so you can hear everything again.

> Which sounds were harder for you to turn down?
> Did you hear any sounds at the end that you didn't originally hear in the beginning?
> Was it easier or harder to hear things with your eyes closed?

PLAY THAT RADIO

CRACK THE MUSIC CODE

Use the notes on the staff to decode the message below.

N e v e r   e a t   e g g s   ON   C A B B A G E   A T   A   C A F E

Listening to the same playlist over and over again on a road trip can get really old, really fast. Switch things up a bit with a few music games!

RADIO ROULETTE

Have someone in the car press the scan button on the radio, and then, when a station comes on, no one can press scan again for at least two songs ... even if you don't like the music! If anyone in the car can correctly guess the name of the artist on the second song that plays, that person then gets to pick the station for the next two songs. If no one guesses correctly, you have to press scan again.

SONG PSYCHIC

Have someone in the front of the car turn the volume of the radio down all the way. Then everyone in the car picks a word or phrase and announces it to all the other passengers. Turn the volume back up, and the first person to hear the word or phrase they chose gets one point. The first person to three points gets to pick the next station.

HUM IT

Turn the radio off for this game. One person starts by humming a song that most people in the car would know. Whoever guesses the song first becomes the next hummer.

RAP STAR

You get to be the musical entertainment for this game. Use your rhyming skills to create a freestyle rap with the other passengers in the car. Have the first person look out the window and say the first thing they see, hear, or smell to start the rap. Then have the next person come up with a line that rhymes. For instance, person one says, "I see a dumpster; bet it smells real bad," and the next person could respond, "I don't wanna know what food they had."

ANSWERS ON PAGE 94

CROSSWORD PUZZLE

ACROSS

3 The area around a vehicle that cannot be directly seen by the person driving.

5 Located on the front and back of a vehicle, this prevents damage in a minor accident.

8 Vehicle function that allows the driver to release their foot from the pedal while still maintaining speed.

12 Occasionally needs a jump start.

15 Dashboard gauge that measures the speed of the vehicle.

16 Some say this purrs, but it always turns over before it runs.

17 All-_____Drive.

18 Piping system that removes gases from the engine.

19 Type of fuel often used with large trucks and military vehicles.

22 Flashing light that indicates which direction a driver is intending to turn.

23 Engine lubricant.

24 Parking, emergency, and anti-lock are all types of _____.

25 Also known as petrol.

DOWN

1 Window on the roof of a vehicle.

2 Decorative cover over the wheel.

4 Long panel in the front row of a vehicle; its name dates back to the 19th century when a carriage added one to keep mud from being "dashed" onto passengers.

6 Helps keep the engine from overheating with the use of coolant.

7 Always check your rear-view _____ before driving.

9 Gearbox that turns an engine's power into something the car can use. Can be either manual or automatic.

10 Instrument on the dashboard that measures the distance a vehicle has traveled.

11 Buckles you in.

13 Minor accident: _____ bender.

14 Start switch.

20 Liquid that rhymes with tool.

21 This automatically inflates during a collision.

ANSWERS ON PAGE 93

DAILY JOURNAL

Imagine you live in the town you're staying in tonight and write out what a normal day looks like for you there. What do your friends look like? Where do you all hang out? What do you do for fun?

"A *good* TRAVELER has NO FIXED PLANS and IS NOT INTENT ON *arriving.*"

—LAO TZU

Chapter Six

TRAVEL LOG

Date: _____

Today we started in _____
NAME OF CITY

and traveled _____ miles to _____ .
OF MILES   DESTINATION CITY

My favorite stop was:

DRAWING of the DAY:

FAVORITE Food OF THE DAY:

TODAY'S Weather:

Highlight OF THE DAY:

LEARN TO WRITE IN *Code*

What if you could write a postcard to yourself that no one else could read? Well, you can! These secret codes are easy to learn if you know how to crack them. Pick out one code you like and then write a secret message to yourself about your trip on a store-bought postcard. Mail the postcard to your home address and see if you can crack the code once you return home from the trip.

RULE OF SECONDS

Start by leaving a space between the letters as you write out your message, stopping when you reach exactly halfway through the message. Now fill in the empty spaces you just created with the remaining letters of your message. When you read it, you'll only read every second letter starting at the first letter, and when you finish the line, start again with the letters you missed. For example: The message "ARE WE THERE YET" would start as "A_R_E_W_E_T_H" and then become "AERREEWYEETTH."

PIGPEN CODE

Use the grids on the left to write in this code. Each letter is represented by the lines around it. For example, TRIP would be written as

A	B	C
D	E	F
G	H	I

J	K	L
M	N	O
P	Q	R

S / T / U / V

W / X / Y / Z

HALF-ABET

Write the alphabet in the grid below, A–M on top and N–Z on bottom. Swap the letters above and below each other to write out a code. In other words, A will become N and N will now become A. For example: HELLO becomes URYYB.

A	B	C	D	E	F	G	H	I	j	k	l	m
N	Q	P	Q	R	S	T	U	V	W	X	Y	Z

YBIR

REVERSE, REVERSE!

Simply write out your message backwards, or should I say: "Sdrawkcab egassem rouy tuo etirw ylp

Hi! I'm Maggie

CREATE YOUR OWN

Use the grid below to create a symbol, letter, or marking that represents each letter of the alphabet.

A	B	C	D	E	F	G	H	I	J	K	L	M

N	O	P	Q	R	S	T	U	V	W	X	Y	Z

TOP SECRET

Imagination STATION

Imagine what the world outside your window would look like to a giant. Would the hills be bouncy like a trampoline? Would they make bouquets of trees for Mother's Day gifts? What would the world look like to a teeny tiny person? Could they even see you over the blades of grass? Would they ride on birds like horses?

The world's tallest grass is called "Dragon Bamboo" and it can grow taller than 100 feet.

The highest any human has ever bounced on a trampoline was 22 feet and 1 inch in the air.

Logo Quest

Every automotive company has its own logo. Some of the logos tell a story about the company and some are just designed to look cool. Go on a logo quest and draw in the logos for the car companies listed below as you see them driving by.

ACURA	AUDI	BMW	CHEVROLET

DODGE	FORD	HONDA	HYUNDAI
	Ford		

LEXUS	MAZDA	MERCEDES-BENZ	NISSAN

SUBARU	TESLA	TOYOTA	VOLKSWAGEN

VOLVO	_____	_____	DESIGN YOUR OWN

Design Your Own CAR

Did you know the youngest concept car designer was just 10 years old when he was offered a job from two major car companies? Concept cars don't have to work; they just show off what styles, features, and technologies could be possible for the future of the car industry. Use the space below to design your own concept car ... and remember to load it up with tons of cool features!

Would you rather have a car that ...

FLOATS *or* **FLIES**
[CIRCLE ONE]

IS ECO-FRIENDLY
or **SUPER-FAST**
[CIRCLE ONE]

CAN TALK *or* **DRIVE ITSELF**
[CIRCLE ONE]

THINGS I'VE DONE
So Far

How does your road trip add up? Give yourself points for the things you've done so far and then add up your list to see how close you're getting to the perfect road trip score! Remember, this game doesn't end until you arrive back home.

TOTAL SCORE:

Tried something new. *3 points*

Waved at another car. *2 points*

Held my breath through a tunnel. *1 point*

Gave away something of mine to someone I didn't know. *3 points*

Shopped for souvenirs. *1 point*

Went for a hike. *2 points*

Played a road trip game. *1 point*

Won at the Alphabet Game. *2 points*

Read a book. *2 points*

Went swimming. *2 points*

Fell asleep in the car. *1 point*

Honked the car horn. *1 point*

Used a map. *2 points*

Bought food at a gas station. *1 point*

Attended a local event (i.e., farmers market, carnival, parade, etc.). *3 points*

Stayed overnight in a hotel. *1 point*

Camped outside. *2 points*

Offered to take a picture for another family. *3 points*

Watched a movie. *1 point*

Danced in the car. *2 points*

Sang along to my favorite song. *1 point*

Learned something new. *3 points*

Felt the wind in my hair. *2 points*

Saw a sunrise. *1 point*

Laughed until my belly hurt. *2 points*

Took a picture with a roadside attraction. *3 points*

LESS THAN 10 POINTS
Um, have you been sleeping this whole time?

11–30 POINTS
Hey, sounds like you're having fun so far! You're on your way to the best road trip ever.

31–47 POINTS
Wow, you're so close to having the perfect road trip! You must be a road trip pro, but there's still time to try to up your score!

48 POINTS
You did it! You just had the perfect road trip! Not many people know how to have as much fun as you do. You are the ultimate road tripper!

The Alphabet Game

Never heard of The Alphabet Game?! It's easy to play. You just search for letters of the alphabet anywhere outside the car. Each player must find the letters in alphabetical order, and only one player can use a letter from the same word. The first player to find Z wins!

73

MATCH THE SIGNS

Draw a line to match each road sign to its meaning.

No U-Turn
Added Lane Warning
One Way
No Entry
Danger
Intersection
Yield
Parking
No Through Road
Railroad Crossing Ahead
Round About
Warning: Hill Ahead
Slippery When Wet
Pedestrian Crossing
Hospital
Right Lane Ends
Keep Right
Construction Workers Present
No Left Turn
No Parking
Two-Way Traffic Ahead
Deer Crossing
Narrow Bridge Ahead
Tent Camping

ANSWERS ON PAGE 93

DAILY JOURNAL

There's a famous quote about travel from the leader of the Duwamish and Suquamish tribes, Chief Seattle: "Take only memories, leave only footprints." What do you think Chief Seattle meant when he said that? Which specific memories from this trip do you plan to keep?

"The World is a book, and those who do not travel read only one page."

— Saint Augustine

Chapter
Seven

TRAVEL LOG

Date: _____

Today we started in _____
NAME OF CITY

and traveled _____ miles to _____ .
OF MILES   DESTINATION CITY

My favorite stop was:

DRAWING of the DAY:

FAVORITE *Food* OF THE DAY:

TODAY'S *Weather*:

Highlight OF THE DAY:

ROAD TRIP *Safari*

Write down all the animals you see today: birds, dogs, deer, or even roadkill.
Write down what you find and then try to give those animals new names!

ANIMALS	NEW NAMES
_____	_____
_____	_____
_____	_____
_____	_____
_____	_____
_____	_____
_____	_____
_____	_____

Play It : HEY COW!

Shout "Hey cow!" out the window when
you pass by a field of cows.
The number of cows that look back at
you after you yell is the number of
points you get for that round.

CLICK IT!

You probably took a lot of photos on this trip, and that's awesome! Pictures are a great way to remember the places you've been and the moments you've enjoyed most. Unfortunately, sometimes pictures get lost or deleted, so it always helps to back up your memories with a mental picture.

Snapping a mental picture is easy, you simply take in all the sights, sounds, smells, tastes, and feels around you for a few seconds, and then close your eyes and try to recreate everything you just saw with your memory. Open your eyes again, and then blink them closed once more. CLICK! You have a picture in your memory that you can pull up anytime you want to see it!

Now think of your favorite photo or mental picture that you took and draw it from memory here.

MEMORY BOOST

Do you have a hard time remembering names? Use the NAME acronym and never forget a name again.

N otice how the name sounds and try emphasizing different parts of it in your head. For instance, Billy could be bil-LY or BIL-ly.

A sk to hear the name again or ask the person where their name came from.

M ention the person's name at least three times while talking to them. "Nice to meet you Billy. Where are you from Billy? Hey Billy, do you have any pets?"

E xamine the most noticeable feature on the person's face, whether it's large ears, freckles, or even a bright eye color.

TEST YOUR Trucker IQ

Driving a semi-truck requires a special license and a special knowledge of the road. Circle the answers to the questions below and tally them up to find your trucker IQ.

1. Truck drivers are not allowed to drive more than ___ hours in a single day.
   a. 11   b. 8   c. 3   d. 24

2. When you stick your arm out the window and pump it up and down, a truck driver will
   a. slow down   b. speed up   c. honk the horn   d. swerve

3. The typical eighteen-wheeler can carry 80,000 pounds. That's roughly the same as
   a. 500 people   b. 16 elephants   c. 800,000 hot dogs   d. all of the above

4. During one year (365 days), the average trucker spends this many days on the road.
   a. 15   b. 300   c. 365   d. 200

5. To run a mile around a semi-truck, you'd have to run this many laps around it.
   a. 10   b. 1   c. 32   d. 102

6. When a semi-truck is driving without the trailer attached, it's called
   a. bobtailing   b. semi-naked   c. fishtailing   d. a truck

7. Showers at gas stations are reserved only for truck drivers.
   a. true   b. false

8. Most states require that semi-trucks can't be taller than
   a. 13'6"   b. 8'   c. 20'   d. 6'

9. The average semi-truck traveling at 55 MPH needs 512 feet to come to a complete stop, that's the same length as
   a. almost 2 football fields   b. 1,024 hot dogs   c. 89 people   d. all of the above

10. Ten percent of all semi-trucks are owned by the drivers. A new semi-truck can cost up to
    a. $15   b. $500,000   c. $50,000   d. $5,000

TOTAL: _____

ANSWERS ON PAGE 94

0–2	3–6	7–10
CORRECT ANSWERS: Maybe it's time for you to head back to trucker school.	**CORRECT ANSWERS:** Hmm, I guess you're "semi" smart.	**CORRECT ANSWERS:** Way to go! You're ready for the road.

RIDDLE ME THIS!

There was a truck driver going the wrong way on a one-way street. Two police officers saw him but neither stopped him. Why did the police officers not stop him?

ANSWER ON PAGE 94

WHAT I MISS

It's totally normal to miss things from home while you're traveling. The comfort of your bed, the smell of your sheets, or sometimes even the sweet taste of the water from your faucet can seem like distant memories when you're gone, but soon enough you'll be back home and it will be the things from your travels you miss! Think of 10 things you miss the most about home and write them in Column 1. Then ask someone else in the car to list their top 10 things they miss about home and write their answers in Column 2.

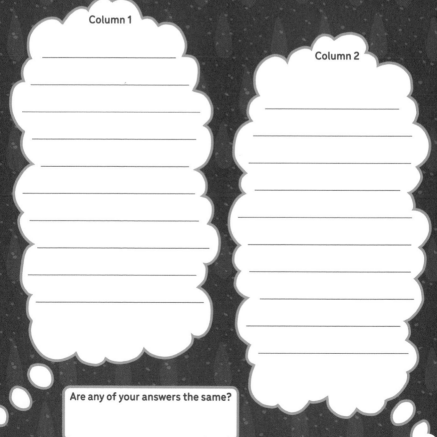

Column 1

Column 2

Are any of your answers the same?

Roadside RESTORATIONS

An abandoned shopping mall in Rhode Island was turned into an apartment building, an old train station was transformed into a private home in New York, and all over North America, people are creating homes inside everything from empty grain silos to abandoned firehouses.

If you had to pick one building to live in that you've seen or driven past on this trip, what would it be? Draw it here.

CAR MAZE

Help the car get home.

SOLUTION ON PAGE 93

BRAIN TEASERS

Solve these Rebus puzzles by using the clues in the box to decipher the word, phrase, or saying they're trying to convey.

TRAIL ITLRA ARTLI LAIRT **PUZZLE 1**	**ROBUMPAD** **PUZZLE 2**	STUCK U **PUZZLE 3**	___ PASS PEDESTRIAN **PUZZLE 4**	ALL ALL WORLD ALL ALL **PUZZLE 5**
BIDDEN BIDDEN ROAD BIDDEN BIDDEN **PUZZLE 6**	J U S T **PUZZLE 7**	**WAY** **PUZZLE 8**	T__RN **PUZZLE 9**	STORM TH **PUZZLE 10**
HAIRPIN **PUZZLE 11**	**TRAVEL** **CCCCCC** **PUZZLE 12**	e go go **PUZZLE 13**	R O A D S R O A D S **PUZZLE 14**	WAY THE TRIP **PUZZLE 15**
STATESSTATESSTATES STATESSTATESSTATES STATESSTATESSTATES **PUZZLE 16**	shield **PUZZLE 17**	LI **PUZZLE 18**	TIRE **PUZZLE 19**	4S9A3F8E1T5Y2 **PUZZLE 20**
once 10:30am **PUZZLE 21**	REST/ROOM **PUZZLE 22**	AIR **PUZZLE 23**	T O W N **PUZZLE 24**	LOAD **PUZZLE 25**
FEN DER **PUZZLE 26**	THHAENRGE **PUZZLE 27**	CTRL **PUZZLE 28**	STREET TEERTS **PUZZLE 29**	TAES DRIVER **PUZZLE 30**

ANSWERS ON PAGE 94

Date: _____

DAILY JOURNAL

Go back and re-read your journal entry from page 19. Was the trip what you expected? Why or why not?

"It's a funny thing COMING HOME. You realize nothing changes. Everything *looks* the same, *feels* the same, even *smells* the same. You realize what's changed is *you*."

—F. SCOTT FITZGERALD

AT HOME

TRAVEL HOST

Travel shows are so popular because people love to hear about awesome adventures, crazy foods, and funny mishaps. As long as the host isn't braggy or boastful, of course!

Write down 5 things you would tell a friend about your trip.

 1

 2

 3

 4

5

Now call your friend or invite them over to talk about it!

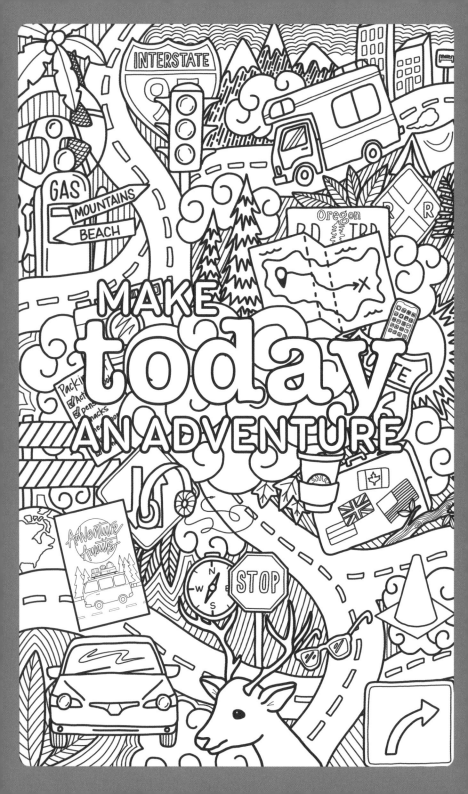

WHERE TO NEXT?

"My favorite thing to do is go where I've never been." — Diane Arbus

Now that you are home from your trip, where do you want to go next?
Follow this decision tree to find out which vacation is right for you!

FREE SPACE

Doodle
+ DRAW

NOTES and
Memories

TICKET STUBS leaves mementos

ANSWERS

WORD SEARCH, page 34

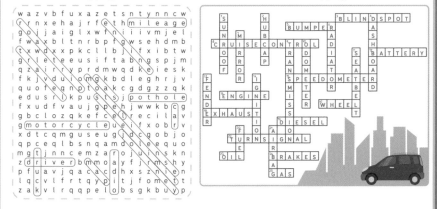

CROSSWORD PUZZLE, page 64

MATCH THE SIGNS, page 74

No U-Turn
Added Lane Warning
One Way
No Entry
Danger
Intersection
Yield
Parking
No Through Road
Railroad Crossing Ahead
Round About
Warning: Hill Ahead
Slippery When Wet
Pedestrian Crossing
Hospital
Right Lane Ends
Keep Right
Construction Workers Present
No Left Turn
No Parking
Two-Way Traffic Ahead
Deer Crossing
Narrow Bridge Ahead
Tent Camping

CAR MAZE, page 83

ANSWERS

BRAIN TEASERS, page 84

1. Trail mix
2. Bump in the road
3. Stuck in the middle with you
4. Pedestrian underpass
5. All around the world
6. Forbidden road
7. Just around the corner
8. Highway
9. No U-turn
10. Thunderstorm
11. Hairpin curve
12. Travel overseas
13. Ready to go
14. Crossroads
15. The trip is under way
16. United States
17. Windshield
18. License
19. Flat tire
20. Safety in numbers
21. Once upon a time
22. Restroom break
23. Air bag
24. Downtown
25. Wide load
26. Fender bender
27. Hang in there
28. Cruise control
29. Two-way streets
30. Back seat driver

Imagination Station, page 23: UNSCRAMBLE ANSWERS: stop sign, drive, journey, passenger

Color Quest, page 25: RIDDLE ANSWERS: 1. A stamp, 2. Glass. All greenhouses are made of glass, 3. They're the same; a pound is a pound, 4. A river, 5. Footprints, 6. An earthworm, 7. A map

Design Your Own License Plate, page 31: ANSWERS: Pee before we go, Later bro, Easy rider, To see stars, Gee you are slow, I love pizza, Crazy for you

Seatback Storyteller, page 42: RIDDLE ME THIS ANSWER: The library!

You Ate What, page 52: MENU ANSWERS: 1-C, 2-E, 3-B, 4-J, 5-D, 6-G, 7-A, 8-F, 9-H, 10-I

Imagination Station, page 53: WHAT'S DIFFERENT ANSWERS: (1) Large lollipop is green in left image and yellow in the right image, (2) Brown chocolate bar in right image is missing the "E" in CHOCOLAT, (3) Small peppermint candy is red in left image and green in the right image, (4) Fruit chew candy is pink in left image and light brown in the right, (5) Blue lollipop stick is shorter in left image.

Play That Radio, page 63: CRACK THE MUSIC CODE ANSWER: never eat eggs on cabbage at a café

Test Your Trucker IQ, page 80: ANSWERS: 1-A, 2-C, 3-D, 4-B, 5-C, 6-A, 7-false, 8-A, 9-D, 10-B; RIDDLE ANSWER: He was walking

ABOUT THE *Author*

KRISTY ALPERT

Kristy Alpert is an award-winning travel journalist whose quest for adventure has led her everywhere from the Bwindi Impenetrable Forest in Uganda, where she trekked to see the silverback gorillas, to Antarctica, where she took part in the "polar plunge" after days spent observing penguins along the penguin highway.

She is a mom and a self-proclaimed "Master of Boredom Busters" after spending years working and traveling with youth, but it is her training as a certified yoga instructor and professional traveler that led her to write a book that aims to inspire the next generation to use all of their senses so they can have a truly memorable journey.

Her favorite road trip partner is her husband Mark, who always picks the best music and makes her laugh harder than anyone else. See more of her writing in *Esquire*, *Cosmopolitan*, *Men's Health*, *Food & Wine*, and *AFAR*, or find out where she's off to next at www.kristyalpert.com.

ABOUT THE *Illustrator*

TAMIKO MURMAN

Tamiko graduated from Harvard in 2004 with a BA in Psychology before attending the Summer Institute at the Stanford Graduate School of Business, but it was during an internship at an aerospace company that she received her formal training as a graphic designer and font specialist. Tamiko opened her own design business, Designs by Tamiko, in 2001, creating custom designs, logos, and intricate hand lettering for clients including Vince Camuto, Swoozie's, The Cancer Support Community, The Global Health Force (a nonprofit she helped create that provides medical supplies and services to underserved populations around the world), and more.

Tamiko was raised in southern California and currently resides in a suburb of Portland with her husband and three champion, road trippin' kids. View more of her work at www.designsbytamiko.com.

ABOUT *You*!

You're the author of your adventures, and we want to hear more about you and the places you love most.

Write your own author bio in the space below.

YOUR *Ultimate* ROAD TRIP

Favorite road trip snacks?

Favorite road trip song?

Favorite game on the road?

5 *Places*
YOU WANT TO SEE SOMEDAY

1.

2.

3.

4.

5.